Dealing with Your Implicit Racism

For black people and anti-racism activists

SEFUNMI OLADUMIYE

ISBN-13: 9781521090008

DEDICATION

This book is dedicated to anyone who has believed the lie that they are inferior and ugly. May you come to realize that you have a choice in what you believe, and may you choose to see yourself through the beauty of God's eyes.

CONTENTS

ACKNOWLEDGMENTS

Writing this book has been quite an experience for me, and I couldn't have done it without Jesus. I want to say thank you Lord for giving me the idea of this book. I am grateful for the strength you gave me to remain in front of the laptop and persevere during those early days when I struggled to find the words to write.

I would like to thank my mom for the use of her laptop, for reading the book, and encouraging me. A big thank you to my editors, Seyi Oladumiye and Tobi Oladumiye, who patiently sat down and worked out the kinks in my manuscript. I would also like to thank all others who unknowingly helped me get this book published, and all who read this book in advance and posted reviews on it. God bless you.

.

1 INTRODUCTION

I did not write this book to prove that racism towards black people exists, so if you are reading this book for that purpose, then you will be disappointed. I wrote this book to help those who already know that racism exists fight against implicit (and explicit) racism in their own lives. Most people in this category are the ones who often spend time explaining racism to others, but they rarely give advice on how to fight against racism on a personal level. I believe this is because they themselves struggle with racism in their own lives and don't have the answers on how to fight it. This previous statement might shock some people because it is easy to think that your first hand experience with racism or your ability to recognize racism makes you immune to having racist thoughts, beliefs, and actions. In the following chapters, I will explain, using my own personal experience, why no one is immune to anti-black racism.

There are a few definitions out there of racism, but I will be using a very basic definition that I believe is fundamental to any other detailed explanation of racism. Many people may see racism as an inherent trait that you are born with, and I think this is one of the reasons why some people feel so condemned when they are accused of racism. Hopefully, this book will help to remove the stigma that is associated with racism by explaining exactly where it comes from.

As you read this book, you will begin to understand how implicit racism works inside of a person. This knowledge will further explain why Blacks and anti-racism activists can also be prejudiced and discriminate against black people. In chapter six, I will further elaborate by using everyday examples.

A lot of black people and anti-racism activists frequently speak out against racism, but the problem is that telling people to stop being racist is as effective as telling a drug addict to stop using drugs. Just because people know something is wrong does not mean they also know how to stop doing that thing. Some things need to be broken down into comprehensible steps that people can follow. That is why in chapter seven I put forth clear and concise racism fighting techniques that have worked for me over the years and which I continue to use to this day.

I am writing this book with a focus on anti-black racism for two reasons: firstly, I have experienced it, and secondly, I believe that anti-black racism is the most prevalent form of racism. This is not to say that other groups of people do not face prejudice and discrimination or have not faced the same kind of problems. I am well aware that other 'races', ethnicities, nationalities, women, and people with disabilities also face discrimination. What I say and teach in this book can be applied to combat prejudice towards any group of people. It can also be used to combat other issues that have nothing to do with 'race'. Furthermore, throughout this book, you will see the word 'race' placed in quotation marks. This is because while this book deals with racism, 'races' do not exist genetically. It is a social construct that some countries have used to describe people, but there isn't any real scientific evidence to back it up[1] Nevertheless, this social construct has created certain realities for different groups of people. And in order to describe these realities, I need to use the word 'race'. However, by the end of this book, I hope to help people really question the notion of 'race' and start to truly see and treat each and every human being as an individual.

2 ABOUT YOU

You may not think that you are a racist or that you have any implicit racism. I think that one thing most people have in common is that they all think other people are racist; they never see racism as also being a part of them. This applies to black people who have experienced racism first hand. Below, I have described three kinds of people that I am writing this book for; however, you might find yourself in more than one of these descriptions.

Person 1- You are an anti-racism activist
You are aware that black people sometimes get treated differently, often in a negative manner. You are actively involved on social media and in the society decrying racism. You are aware of certain privileges other 'races' receive. And you do not consider yourself to be racist.

Person 2- You are a black person or of black descent
You have experienced racism first hand. You are active on social media and in the society speaking out against racism. You are familiar with the phrase 'institutionalized racism'; therefore, you believe that black people cannot be racist.

Or you may believe that racism goes both ways. You feel that black people complain too much about racism, and you do not think of yourself as a racist.

Person 3- You are in between
You are not active on social media decrying racism, but you believe that black people are sometimes treated differently. You do not really understand terms like institutionalized racism or white privilege. You believe that you are a good person, and you try to treat everyone equally.

No condemnation
I believe that no matter what your color or beliefs are, most people in this day

and age have implicit prejudice, especially towards Blacks. In the following chapters, I will explain why I believe this is so. I am not writing this book to throw anyone under the bus, or to condemn anyone; given my experience, which you will find out in the next chapter, I am in no position to pick up the first stone or any stone for that matter and throw it at anyone. I am writing this book to unveil how implicit racism works, and what can be done to overcome it.

3 ABOUT ME

I come from the most populous black nation in the world: Nigeria. The practices of 'race' and color identification are generally foreign to us. It is not because we do not see color, nor understand the notion of different types of people. We rather identify and distinguish ourselves on the basis of our numerous ethnic groups which include Yoruba, Igbo, Hausa, and Calabar to name a few. From my experience, it appears that there is not a comprehensive understanding of the concept of racism. Some have argued that it is just an obstacle that can be overcome through hard work and good behavior.

The move
My family left Nigeria and moved to another country when I was around seven years old. This was when my journey with racism began. For the first time in my life, I was exposed to people on the street calling me and my family members names like nigger, monkey, slave, black, Africa, and ugly. In some salons, hairdressers would make fun of my hair and skin color. At the first international school I attended, some white and mixed 'race' teachers and schoolmates just seemed to hate my guts for no reason and would verbally (and once physically) abuse me without provocation. I had no idea why this was happening. I saw their behavior as the acts of people who had problems; I did not see myself as being the problem. I think one of the reasons why I did not internalize their negative behavior towards me was because I was surrounded by other black Africans like myself. We were friends with each other, and we played together. It was among these black Africans that my identity as an African was formed. Being around them was like a wall of protection that shielded me from internalizing the racism and discrimination of some teachers and peers.

The fall of the wall

I changed schools around the age of eleven and moved to another international school where there was not a strong black African presence. For the first time, I had no wall to shield me from the racist views and treatment that came from some students and some teachers. However, the mistreatment I experienced at my new school was nothing like the confrontational, angry, and direct mistreatment of my former school. This mistreatment was more subtle. Instead of yelling at and verbally and physically abusing me, some teachers would smile at me while treating me like I was lazy, aggressive, and a cheater. I was none of these things. They would write things in my report card about how I was disrespectful to them, inconsiderate of others, and lacked organization and leadership skills. All these assessments left me seriously perplexed. I wondered how I was inconsiderate to others. How many times was I disrespectful to them that earned me poor marks in respect? What opportunities were available to an eleven year old to show leadership skills without being called a sissy by some teachers (which had happened to me in my former school)? And no matter how hard I worked in some subjects that were considered 'easy As' for all students, I just would not get grades above a certain level. This was despite the fact that I was without a doubt more knowledgeable in these subjects than the students who were given higher marks. Even some of these very students would gasp in awe at the quality of my work. This mistreatment I speak of does not refer to the few occasions when I was rightfully reprimanded by some teachers for wrong behavior or the times when I was given and justly deserved low grades. It however refers to some teachers' negative perception of me that made me wonder, "What's the problem? What did I do? Did you have to treat me that way?"

At the same time, instead of calling me ugly, some schoolmates would play games of Truth or Dare and would dare some guy to tell me he thought I was beautiful. (If you have played Truth or Dare, then you know that you are usually dared to do something horrific). In addition to this, small requests on my part from some schoolmates were met with a lecture, refusals, or huffs and puffs of inconvenience, while another person could also make the same request right after me and would be warmly given. Also, some schoolmates who were not in my grade and who I had never spoken to or even thought about would treat me like I was their enemy. This is not to say that I was a saint; it is just to highlight the fact that I noticed a recurring trend of unwarranted negativity from certain schoolmates that left me perplexed.

Identity crisis

By the age of twelve, I began to ask myself, "Why me? Why was I being treated like this by some schoolmates? Was I a bad person?" I assessed my behavior and came to the conclusion that I could not be that bad since my classmates had no qualms asking me for help. One thing I had learnt from a young age was that people didn't ask a mean person for help unless they absolutely had to. And if they did, they would do so with some trepidation. Classmates showed no signs of trepidation when asking me for help. So what was the problem, I wondered?

I began to look around my class, and I noticed that a few other classmates received similar treatment to varying degrees. I observed that we all had a common feature-it was the color of our skin. We were all black Africans.

I don't want to be black
That was the moment I realized I was black; and at that moment, a lot of the negative views that people generally have about Blacks just got downloaded into my head. I instantly understood that as a black person, a lot of people viewed me as ugly, disgusting, repulsive, dirty, and any negative thing that applied in any situation. For example, if being quiet in a classroom situation was considered bad, then the black kids in that classroom were probably the quiet ones. On the other hand, if being loud in a classroom was considered bad, then the black kids in that classroom were probably the loud ones. So, no matter the situation, black people were always the first suspects.

In hindsight, I see that I just accepted these beliefs as the truth. It never crossed my mind to question them. I was viewed as repulsive and ugly, so I believed that all black people including myself were repulsive and ugly. Prior to this realization, I had believed I was pretty; this belief was something that was very important to me. Therefore, it crushed me to accept this belief. Unfortunately, instead of rejecting these negative views, I rejected the color of my skin. I did not want to be black. I started to pray every day for God to make me a white person because I saw that everyone, whether they were white, Asian, black, and mixed race, treated white people better. For many months, I seriously believed that God was going to grant my request, but the question that kept coming to my mind was: 'how are you going to explain to your parents going to bed black and waking up white?'Eventually, I realized that God wasn't going to make me white. In my disappointment, I remember saying to God in anger, "It's not fair God! You made all white people pretty, and you made black people ugly!" The moment I said that, an image of a random and average looking white person rose to the surface of my mind contradicting what I had just said. I paused and considered whether I thought this white person was pretty (now keep in mind, this was the mind of a twelve year old going through an identity crisis). I threw the image out of my mind, and I said, "God, it doesn't matter if I'm ugly and white, I'll still be treated better than a black person."

I saw that white people were viewed and treated as superior. So I made up my mind that I was going to marry a white man because if he thought I was beautiful, then I believed everyone else would think so too and ultimately treat me better. Moreover, I viewed white men as handsome and black men as ugly and beastly. Lastly, I needed to have biracial children because in the society I was living in, they were treated just as well as white children. I did not want to have black kids who would suffer similar discrimination like me.

Colorism

Even though I had grudgingly accepted that I was not going to become white, I refused to give up on my quest to be treated better. That was when I became conscious that light skinned black people were treated better than those of a darker hue. So I decided to make my skin lighter because I am dark skinned. I had heard comments about how some black people had gotten lighter when they went to regions that did not have much sun. Therefore, I created a type of ninja head gear to keep the sun from touching my face during the summer holidays. This attempt was doomed from the start because apparently a radical change in skin tone does not come about by covering one's face. Besides, the head gear was badly crafted, and it really only covered my mouth.

False acceptance

My two attempts at changing the color of my skin had failed. I had run out of ideas. So I decided to accept my skin color out of spite for those who hated it. You know how you decide to like something not because you like it, but because someone you do not like hates it? Well I decided that I was black and proud because there were people who wanted me to be black and ashamed.

I was not black and proud in the least. I was black and ashamed. I saw black men and women as ugly and unattractive (especially darker skinned Blacks). To me, black people had fat, unattractive lips, were disgusting, and were just not worthy. Watching two black people kiss on TV was extremely repulsive to me. When I looked through magazines, I only noticed non-black people; I did not give pictures with black people a second glance, especially those with darker skin. I also was not as respectful towards black and mixed race teachers as I was towards white teachers. If I saw a black woman among white people, I felt ashamed and uncomfortable because I felt like that black woman did not belong. I felt sorry for myself. I had monologues with myself about how people should treat you based on who you were on the inside, not based on your outward appearance. Interestingly, during this time, I also had my first teenage, celebrity crush on a light skinned black rapper. It was intense. I had it all planned out in my 14 year old head. I was going to move to his hometown for my university education, we were going to meet, and I was going to marry him. My dreams of marrying a white man got shelved until I got over this first crush.

Intervention

Around this time, I heard God whisper something into my heart, "You are behaving hypocritical. You want people to judge you by your character, not by the color of your skin, but you judge black people by the color of their skin." I was mortified. Behaving like a hypocrite was a very shameful thing to me, but I knew God was right; I knew my prejudiced thoughts and beliefs about black people, so I decided to make a change. In the following chapters, I will describe what I did to combat racism within myself. With the help of these tools, I was able to change the racist beliefs I had about black people into positive ones.

No more a racist?

You may have read the subtitle of this book and wondered why I said that this book is for black people and anti-racism activists. *We are not the ones who need to stop being racist*, you may think. However, from my story, I think you can see that even though I was a black person, I had racist thoughts, beliefs, and actions towards black people. Furthermore, when you were reading my story, what country did you think my family moved to? A European, Asian, or non-black country? If you thought this, then you were wrong. My family moved to another African country where although the majority of the population are mixed 'race', most would be categorized as Black in many other societies. I have experienced racism from all 'races', Black, White, Asian, and mixed 'race' people included. While black people need to fight against racism directed at us from other people, we also need to understand that we ourselves are just as susceptible to racist beliefs about black people as any other 'race'. We can internalize these beliefs and use them to discriminate against ourselves, especially against darker skinned Blacks, as was done to me and as I eventually did.

Over the years, I have become more knowledgeable on racism. I am also active on social media, sharing and discussing articles related to racism. Therefore, you might think that I no longer have to fight negative views about black people or views that put white people on a pedestal. If this is what you think, then you would be wrong again. While I am no longer dominated by explicit racist beliefs about Blacks and Whites, a few racist ideas still try to creep into my mind. I call this implicit racial bias because I am not immediately conscious of their effects on me until my actions reveal them to me. I combat these implicit racist views with the same techniques I fought the explicit ones. Black people and anti-racism activists of all colors need to know how to identify and reject implicit racist ideas before they become biases. Although I believe everyone needs to have this knowledge, I addressed this book to these two groups of people because I personally feel they will be more open to hear what I have to say. Nevertheless, this book can be used by anyone.

*

Let us begin by defining what racism is, where it comes from, and how it operates.

4 THE WHAT AND WHERE OF RACISM

For the purposes of this book, here are the brief definitions that I will be using to define the words prejudice, discrimination, and racism.

Prejudice is when you have an opinion or feeling about someone or something that is not based on any fact or experience[1]. For example, I believed all black men were violent, even though I had never actually experienced violence at the hands of black men. Prejudiced opinions may be explicit or implicit, meaning you may be aware that you have them, or you may not be aware that you have them. In my case, I was explicitly aware that I had these thoughts and beliefs about black men.

Discrimination is when you take actions based on the prejudiced opinions you have[2]. These actions can also be explicit or implicit. For example, I was not as respectful to some black and mixed 'race' teachers as I was to white ones, and a part of me was slightly aware of this.

There are many detailed definitions of racism; however, the basic dictionary definition I will be using for this book defines **Racism** as the belief that a group of people or 'race' possesses certain intrinsic traits that make them superior or inferior to others. This belief creates prejudice against the 'inferior race' and leads to antagonism and discriminatory actions against them[3]. It also gives unearned privileges to the 'race' that is considered 'superior'. Growing up, the only definition I had of racism was that you were a racist if you hated and mistreated ***all*** black people, but as you can see from my experience, I did not hate black people; I just saw us as inferior to Whites. The belief that one 'race' is superior or inferior can also be implicit or explicit. Few black people will say that they believe Blacks are inferior, but if one was to examine our thoughts, words, and actions, we may see a slight pattern of colorism revealing that some of us do unconsciously believe this. **Colorism** is when people within a 'race' experience prejudice and discrimination based on the lightness or darkness of their skin tone[4]. Colorism gives preference to those who are of a lighter skin tone and to those with features that are less black and closer to white. It is sometimes portrayed as if colorism is an intra-racial problem, meaning it is only Blacks or Asians who prefer lighter skinned members of their 'race' to darker skinned members. However, colorism is an offshoot of racism because it views those who are closer to white as superior. Therefore, anyone can engage in colorism.

Finally, prejudice, discrimination, and racism do not necessarily manifest every single time we interact with black people because other factors besides 'race' can affect how we view or treat a black person at any given time. For example: despite my negative views of black men, I still had positive interactions with them because we went to the same school and played and had discussions together. I even nurtured a passionate crush on a black rapper and wanted to marry him because I was a teenager whose hormones were raging, and the guy was light skinned and famous. Also, we may have prejudiced beliefs about Blacks in a certain area, but exclude our black friends from those beliefs because we know and like them. Furthermore, other factors can overlap with racism, meaning both of them can operate at the same time. For example: people may treat a black person badly because he/she is *poor* and *black*. Racism is just one factor among others in human interactions. A lack of understanding of this prevented me from recognizing racism towards me from some teachers.

Where does racism come from?

Some people think that racism is a biological defect which certain 'races' suffer from. Thankfully, that is not the case. **I believe racism is learned ideas and beliefs that are taught through: Culture, Society, and the Media**. There may be other avenues that teach racism, but these three are the ones that I have been able to identify. Culture, society, and the media teach racism by explicitly and implicitly transmitting **ideas** through words, images, expressions, likes, dislikes, behavior, and so on.

Culture

According to the website Live Science, "Culture is the characteristics and knowledge of a particular group of people, defined by everything from language, religion, cuisine, social habits, music and arts."[5]

Things and practices that are particular to a certain group of people become their culture. One may not even be aware that these practices are cultural until one goes outside of his/her country and finds out that people do not do things the way it is done 'back home'. Also, they may find out that some of their cultural practices are offensive to others. The problem with culture when dealing with racism is that some cultural traditions carry special memories and have been practiced for such a long time that people no longer know the malicious origins behind them. Therefore, those who practice them usually have no hateful intent. So when someone starts to point out racist things within their cultures and traditions, they take offense because they feel like it is an attack on them and their way of life. For example, in Nigeria, Biracials are called *Half-castes*. When I left Nigeria, I found out about the origins of the word *caste*, and I learned that it was an offensive term; so I stopped using it. However, some Nigerians may reject the idea that it is an offensive term because they have been innocently using it for many years without any malicious intent on their part.

Society

Society, on the other hand, is "**a group of people who share similar values, laws and traditions living in organized communities for mutual benefits.** Members of society often share religions, politics or culture."[6]

People make up societies. People in our places of worship, our schools, our communities, our neighborhoods, our cities, our families, and our political parties are societies. Societies help to shape what we believe in that we tend to accept the ideas that are already in place in our societies. We also tend to keep quiet about the ideas we do not accept for fear of being a lone voice in the society or ostracized from it.

The media

Finally, the media refers to all the different forms of mass communication like television, film, the internet, books, magazines, and advertisements

All the media listed above communicate ideas to us. Even the colorful educational posters in kindergarten classrooms influence us. Finally, movies, TV shows, adverts, and the news media are some of the most powerful tools to transmit ideas into people because of their very visual nature and how entertaining they can be.

The definitions I have used in this chapter are brief in order to give you the general idea of what I will be discussing in this book. Furthermore, while I have listed the three elements that I believe transmit racism, I would also like to point out that there is another element that plays a role in where racism comes from. I believe there is a tendency in human nature to want to be superior to others in all things considered good, whether it's superior in beauty, in country, in love, or in family. This is the reason why competitions happen on this planet; we need to beat people at something. It is like we have this God sized hole within us that needs to be constantly filled with thoughts of worth. We want to be worth something; and we feel that if we are better than others, then we truly are valuable.

*

Before I show you how cultures, societies, and the media implicitly transmit racist ideas, let us see where racist ideas live and how to catch them.

5 THE BATTLE IS IN THE MIND

Now that we know that culture, society, and the media are all transmitting ideas, the question is where are these ideas going? Ideas are going into our minds. We cannot see it happening, but we see the results of these ideas. Ideas are powerful. They change people, build societies, and determine people's beliefs and actions. A great example of this was my belief about the crescent moon. There are many cartoon images of the crescent moon drawn with a face and a smile. These images are for kids of course, but for a long time I subconsciously believed that the crescent moon had a face, a nose, eyes, and a smile like a person. I believe that I was over the age of twenty and in university before it dawned on me that the moon did not have a face like a person, and that those drawings were just comical representations for children. Nevertheless, before I realized my error, I would often gaze at the crescent moon, looking for his smile, convincing myself that I could see it just a little. Those images gave me a ridiculous idea, and I believed this idea and acted on it for a long time, despite my age and the absurdity of the idea. It was ideas that brought about all the inventions that make our lives easier today. All the different forms of government systems that are currently being employed such as democracy, communism, royalty, and military governments are all based on ideas. I started writing this book because an idea about it came into my mind; the more I thought about this idea, the more it began to take shape. Ideas and thoughts are like seeds, and our minds are like fertile ground for these seeds to grow. On a daily basis we are consciously and unconsciously thinking about ideas. These ideas/thoughts can become feelings and beliefs. And feelings and beliefs will in turn lead to actions. There is a verse in the Bible (Proverbs 23:7) that says, "as he thinks in his heart, so is he", so we can summarize that what you think on, you will eventually act on or become.

The importance of repetition

Fortunately, one way to catch a racist idea is to watch out for **repetition**. Unfortunately, repetition is one of the reasons why racist ideas are still able to slip into our minds and direct our thoughts and actions, even though we are anti-racism activists. Nigerian writer, Chimamanda Adichie, did a TED talk entitled *The danger of a single story*.[1] In her speech, she showed how if one story is told repeatedly about something, it becomes the only image or identity people will have of that thing. A single idea has the ability to change thoughts, form beliefs, and change people. Now imagine if that idea is broadcasted again and again. If one dose of that idea does not convince people, then how about ten, a hundred, or a thousand doses of it everyday for the rest of your life? How many people will be able to withstand the effects of that idea? We have all heard the popular phrase: if you repeat something long enough, it will become truth.

Let's say we bring another idea that challenges the first idea, but we only broadcast this new idea once a week. Which idea will have the greatest effect on people, the first or the second? The answer is the first because the first is being repeated many times daily while the second idea is only being repeated once a week. While a non-racist idea can push back the effects of a racist idea, it can only defeat the racist idea if it is broadcasted more or to the same extent as the racist idea.

Here is an example of how repetition can affect us. A few years back, I used to avidly watch a particular action TV show. Every episode had the main characters involved in fierce fight scenes. After some time of watching this show, I began to fantasize about getting involved in physical fights with people and showing off my imaginary fighting skills. I eventually noticed the direction of my thoughts, and I realized that this action show had influenced me. Let me reiterate what happened to me step by step:

- This TV show is transmitting ideas of fighting. It does not explicitly say fighting is cool, it just shows fighting in a cool way with choreographed fight scenes where the heroic main character wins.
- Furthermore, I watch this show frequently *(repetition)*
- Ideas of fighting and fighting being cool are now frequently floating around in my head.
- The desire to fight or rather to copy those cool fight scenes leads me to have aggressive fantasies.
- I believe if I had continued to allow those thoughts/fantasies to hang out in my mind, I would eventually have tried to pick a fight with someone.

Here is another example: As a teenager, I disliked many parts of my body like a lot of teenage girls do. I wanted to change my thighs, face, and knees. I also wanted to lose weight. When I got to university, I started to exercise daily and almost all the dissatisfaction with my body evaporated. I have been generally happy with my body for up to ten years now (of course, there are still a few things I would like to improve, but regardless, I am happy with my body).

A few months back, my housemate started watching a show about people who had body issues, got bad plastic surgery jobs, and had to go back under the knife to fix them. I did not like watching this show, but since we were living in the same house, I would frequently hear what was happening. Many times, I would sometimes go to the living room just to find out what would be the outcome of a particular story. After watching this show for a few weeks, I began to stop and look at my body in the mirror with some mild dissatisfaction. Desires to make 'just a little' modification here and there crept into my mind. This happened for some time until one day I realized that this was out of character for me. I wondered what had brought on the change, and after some serious soul searching, my mind honed in on the culprit: the plastic surgery show.

Here are the series of events:

- The plastic surgery show is transmitting ideas about body dissatisfaction and changing body parts with plastic surgery.
- I am around and would sometimes watch this show once or twice a week (***repetition again***).
- Ideas of body dissatisfaction are now in my thoughts.
- I begin to consider my own body and start to look for things that displease me.
- I find a few things that displease. I am no longer satisfied with my body and want to make some modifications.

From these examples, you can see how repetition is crucial in the spread of an idea. Furthermore, the example above shows that even though I did not like watching that plastic surgery show, I was still influenced by it because I was repeatedly exposed to it and didn't guard the direction of my thoughts. This is important to note because when it comes to combating racism, you need to know that repeated exposure to a racist idea can affect your views of black people, no matter how strong you think your mind is.

*

In the next chapter, I will show you how racist messages are indirectly transmitted through culture, society, and the media.

6 THE TRANSMISSION

The importance of being implicit

Once upon a time, people were directly told on TV and in books that black people were inferior. This was a common belief that was spewed out without shame. Nowadays, due to social and political progress, this type of direct racism is no longer acceptable. Some people have even gotten fired from their jobs just because they said something racist on social media. However, not being able to say racist things openly does not mean that racist beliefs have disappeared. What has happened is that people privately share their racist ideas and beliefs with others who they feel might have the same views as they do. They also share and spread it indirectly through their culture, society, and the media. I believe that one of the reasons why racism is still a problem is because of implicit racist beliefs. The reason these beliefs are powerful is because they are subtle, yet constantly expressed in many different ways. Therefore, they are able to shape people's views of Blacks without you being aware of what is happening. When Blacks protest against things they feel are racist, you may have heard people respond with, "oh, it's just a movie", or "I don't think that is what they were trying to say". The reason people brush aside these grievances is because they have not yet realized how implicit racist messages affect people's behavior; they do not yet understand that it is more than 'just a movie', it is an idea. That is why these implicit messages need to be exposed and expounded on so that people learn how to detect them and have a better understanding of what makes them racist.

I want to point out that we humans have a choice in what we believe. Every implicit racist idea we subscribe to, we chose to believe it even if it was an unconscious choice. You may ask, "How can you say I had a choice if I did not consciously choose?" I say this because a belief is a choice that we make in our minds; nobody has control over our minds to force us to believe anything, not even God. Someone might deceive us into believing an idea, but we still chose to believe it. I do believe that up to a certain point, we are less accountable for things we unconsciously chose to believe when we were children because as children, our minds were still developing, and we were highly impressionable. Nevertheless, after a while, we need to grow up and take responsibility for our beliefs and learn how to guard our minds. When I was younger, I was indirectly told that I was ugly because I was a dark skinned black girl. I did not have to accept that idea, but I did because I did not know that I had a choice. I now see that *I* chose to believe those voices, and that *I* chose to give more weight to their opinion of me than to God's opinion of me and my opinion of myself. When I became a young adult, I had to choose to see myself as beautiful which made me realize that *I* had chosen to see myself as ugly. That is why it is so very important that we are taught how to recognize and deal with implicit ideas so that we can consciously choose what we want to believe. I will now give some examples on how culture, society, and the media spread implicit racist ideas.

CULTURE

Language

Languages and words are a big part of our cultures, societies, and the media. Words are continuously transmitting images and ideas. So how does language transmit racist ideas about black people? Take for example these idioms: *Black sheep, Black market, blacklist, black look, blackout, and blackmail*. If we remove black from all these words, the words that remain are neutral words: *market, sheep, list, look, etc.* The moment you add the word black to these words, they become negative. The English language has designated the word black to describe many negative things. So how about the words **Black people**? You do not have to write books about how there is something wrong with black people. All you have to do is to constantly associate the word black with negative things, and then by default black people are seen in a negative light. This is how an implicit idea works. Nevertheless, I can understand why people would call Blacks black and Whites white even though neither of us are those colors exactly. While I do not believe that this phenomenon had a racist origin, it has not been helpful as black people are constantly associated with negative things.

Other examples include the use of the expressions: **the Dark Continent** and **third world countries** which have been used to describe the African continent and its countries. The phrase **third world country** was formerly used to describe developing nations. The problem with this phrase is that it depicts these types of nations as inferior in everything to so-called **first and second world countries**. People may rightfully argue that developing nations are inferior to developed nations in terms of economic and social development. The problem with this phrase is that it does not say **third world**

country in terms of economic and social development; it just says **third world country**, which is an all encompassing phrase that can also be used to label the people of those nations as inferior.

Furthermore, just like the word *black* has a negative connotation, so does the word *dark*. When we say something is dark, we mean that it has a lot of problems or is depressing. For example, a period in our lives that was full of troubles is described as 'a dark time'. There is no way that our brains are not going to make the connection between these negative phrases and the fact that they are used to describe the continent that has the most amount of black people in the world. There have been non-racist reasons given for the use of these expressions, however, no matter how innocent the reasons are, these phrases still carry a negative connotation, and they are mainly used to describe black countries. The implicit idea that is being sent is that African countries, and black people by default, are inferior and full of problems.

Religion

The Christians of the past and of today have many painted images of God and of Jesus Christ. We also have many images of religious figures from the Bible and angels. The majority of these images are of white Europeans. I personally do not have any problem with whatever color people decide to paint good religious figures. The problem arises when the devil, demons, and bad people in religious texts are painted. While these figures may not look like black people, they tend to have truly black or grey skin, dark features, and wear black/dark robes. I find this trend occurring in Nigeria, and it associates dark skinned people with evil.

In the small Nigerian town that I live in, there is a billboard of a white European Jesus surrounded by children of different 'races', with white children in the majority. I would not have a problem with this billboard if it was in a small town in a European country. However, this is a Nigerian town where there are virtually no white people. Furthermore, in Nigeria, we are surrounded by images of Jesus as white and demons as black skinned or dark. Most Nigerians are probably not bothered by this, but an implicit seed is being planted.

Now imagine a Nigerian boy named Femi, having been exposed to such images including the one on the billboard, moving to a country that is predominantly white, or Asian, or non-Black. Let's say his new Sunday school wants to put on a play about Jesus and asks kids to audition. Maybe Femi likes to act and has proven himself to be a great actor, but before he even says what part he will audition for, another young child quickly says, "Femi, you can't play Jesus cause you're black and Jesus is white, but you can play the devil" (Yes, things like this can happen). Imagine how Femi would feel: excluded, like there was something wrong with his skin color since it makes him ineligible to play Jesus (a good person) but eligible to play the devil (an evil being). All the images he has been exposed to in Nigeria tell him that what this other kid said is correct. The portrayal of the good beings in the Bible as white and the bad beings as black or dark skinned sends a message to everyone that white people are good and black people are evil.

If Nigerian (or black) children and adults come into contact with enough anti-black racist ideas and discrimination, coupled with religious images like these, some of them will start to wonder why they worship a God that 'looks' like people who exclude them and view them as inferior. This has been my experience, and I have heard other black people express unhappiness about this same issue. What racism and discrimination do is to exclude people, to make an exclusive group of privilege that only those who are 'worthy' (meaning: white, non-Black, light skinned, or rich) can enter. Experiencing exclusion due to 'race' makes it easier to notice racial exclusion. This billboard would never have bothered me if I had never come into contact with racism and discrimination. People may say "Why does it matter if Jesus is depicted as white and if there are many white children in the image, aren't there after all some black kids also?" It matters because white people are already put on a pedestal, so in some black people's eyes worshipping a 'white looking' God is like a validation of white superiority. I also think that it would matter to an all white small town in Europe if there was a billboard in their village of a black Jesus surrounded by a majority of black kids with only two white kids, . "You are speaking to us", I believe they would say, "Why aren't you trying to connect with us at our own level, culture, and people?" I also believe it would bother some people to see Jesus as black. They may say that their discomfort is only because it is not historically accurate, but the image of the blue eyed, non-Jewish, European looking Jesus, which is also not historically accurate, would not bother them in the least.

SOCIETY

Behavior

One way societies transmit negative ideas about black people is through people's behavior. We unconsciously notice how people react in certain situations, how people treat others, and how people speak about others. I learnt I was black and that being black was a negative thing through the negative treatment I experienced from some schoolmates. I do not hate those particular schoolmates or teachers from whom I experienced racism because I now understand that the majority of them were just behaving according to what they had been unconsciously taught by the society. And acknowledging my own faults towards others and the moments of kindness that I experienced from these same teachers and students has helped me to forgive. Nevertheless, children listen to and watch their parents and people around them; the behaviors they see and hear will influence their own beliefs and behavior.

Here are some examples of behaviors that can affect a child's perception of black people:

- The things people say around their children or kids in general about black people when they think no one is around to challenge them.
- How they can view and judge white people as individuals, but condemn all black people for the actions of one person, therefore painting all black people as one and the same instead of also treating them as individuals.
- The passing remarks about how ugly some black celebrities are, and only calling biracial or light skinned black people pretty because their colors are closer to that of white people.
- How quick they are to criticize and condemn black people, and how harsh they are in their criticisms, yet slow to criticize and condemn Whites and non-Blacks, and being lenient on them in the same situations.
- How quick they are to jump to a negative conclusion about black people as if the black person in question has consistently done wrong towards them.
- How they only notice when a black person does something bad, but have selective blindness/amnesia when Whites and non-Blacks do the same bad thing, sending a message that black people are the only ones who do wrong.
- How they suspiciously follow black people around a store even though black people may have previously bought hundreds of things from that store.
- How shocked they react when they find out a black person achieved something positive; how they double check to make sure that it is true; and how they try to link some non-black person to the achievement because in their minds black people are not capable of producing good things, at least not by themselves.
- How the success and fame of some black people are attributed to them being members of a cult like the Illuminati or to them being the Anti-Christ, despite the fact that there are many non-black people who are just as (and even more) successful and famous. It is as if in some people's minds, black people cannot achieve these heights without something being 'fishy'.
- How people like to describe black men as 'He is a *big* black man', putting emphasis on the word big, giving the impression that black

men are overly physically strong. This is called 'The big black man syndrome'.*[1]

- How they cross the street or take another exit when they see a black man (or person) approaching because in their minds black people are dangerous.

All these behaviors send implicit messages to children that there is something bad about black people, and that black people are not individuals, but one and the same. Children and teenagers have a developing mind and conscience, a tendency to imitate others, mouths that can run like a tap, and a limited understanding of how the things they say and do can have long term consequences. This means that children will generally accept these implicit ideas without questioning whether it is right or wrong. They will take what they hear and see in private and broadcast it to the world, often in a thoughtless or mean way because they do not understand the gravity of their actions. Eventually, they will grow into adults. They will learn that they need to put a filter over their mouths (some of them at least); they will learn not to be mean (some of them at least); but how will they learn to challenge the implicit ideas they learnt as children when they do not even know they are there? How will they challenge these implicit racist ideas if they are afraid to pry into their unconscious thoughts and reactions because there is such a stigma around racism? Therefore, these racist beliefs will remain within them, operating at an unconscious level and will get passed on to the future generation.

MEDIA

History Books

History and social studies books often broadcast racism by exclusion. I remember learning quite a bit about the Middle Ages, the Renaissance, the French revolution, and other Western European history in international schools when I was growing up. I don't recall ever learning about the black African Empires of Benin, Mali, Ghana, and Songhai. Some of the textbooks we used were called World History, but the majority of the history written within those textbooks was that of white people in the West. If it was American history, then the stories of African Americans were confined to slavery and the civil rights movement. History was presented from a white

---

[1] Interestingly, to better explain how people often refer to black men as big, I came up with the phrase 'The big black man syndrome'. I typed this phrase into Google search and found out that Lawrence Vogelman had already come up with the same phrase to explain the same issue. Check out Lawrence Vogelman's paper on it: **The Big Black Man Syndrome: The Rodney King Trial and the Use of Racial Stereotypes in the Courtroom**

western perspective. For example, the spread of Christianity is presented as something that happened in Europe, but we are not often told that even before it spread through Europe, it had already spread onto the African continent. We are told that Columbus 'discovered' the Americas, but nothing is said about how the people who were living in the Americas before he came also discovered the Americas. The problem with this situation is that it gives the impression that white western history is the most impactful history in the world. Therefore, the implicit message that comes across is that white people are the most important and that they represent the world. I do not deny that white western history has had some impact on the world, such as the Colonial period and the World Wars. But other histories have also impacted the world, and focusing predominantly on one side gives people the wrong impression.

I believe this is why there is a common belief that black Africans do not have any history. I think in some people's minds, the only place black people have in history is that of slavery. While having ancestors who were enslaved is nothing to be ashamed of, it is still something that people view as shameful and inferior because they do not know the stories of these people which would help them recognize their humanity, strength, resilience and intelligence, as well as the need for their histories to be taught. So in people's minds, the history of many black people is an 'inferior' history, a history that is not worth learning. For some other people, black African history starts when white people colonized the continent.

By making white history and people out to be the norm or the standard, these textbooks are indirectly presenting non-Whites as the **Other**. An **Other** is something that is not the norm. What othering does is that it can create a sense of shame. When I was growing up, the mixed 'race' society I was living in held themselves up to be the standard in terms of physical features. White, Asian, and biracials features were also included into this standard, while black features were not. Realizing that I was not a part of the standard, I allowed myself to become ashamed of my black features like my skin color, my nose, my hair, and the color and size of my lips. I believe that a lot of black women like myself have had to combat feelings of shame about the very things that make us different from Whites or from those who are close in features to Whites. Another thing othering does is that it teaches Blacks and other 'races' to question their differences from Whites, and it teaches Whites never to question why they are different from non-white people, but to question why everyone else is different from them.

Finally, I mentioned in Chapter four that human beings have a God sized need to be constantly told that they are valuable, and that they often fill this need by trying to put themselves above others. The implicit message these textbooks send through othering makes it easy for white people (and other 'races' for that matter) to view themselves as superior.

Magazines/articles

I once read two editions of a particular women's magazine that had next to zero images of non-white women in them. I saw nothing wrong with this because I gathered that this magazine was geared towards white women. However, one edition did a special article on: Women who stay in abusive relationships. It had a big title page with those very words, and then when I turned that page, the first image and story in this article were that of a black woman. This immediately struck me as odd. This magazine didn't see fit to include black women in its pages until it decided to publish a negative story. In this magazine, this was the only image the subscribers would see of a black woman, and so it would become a lasting image of black women in their minds (the single story), especially if they didn't have regular contact with black people. With this image came the implicit ideas that black women were in abusive relationships and that black men (because the first conclusion people draw in general (whether it is correct or incorrect) is that black women are married to black men) were abusive, violent, and therefore dangerous. While the stories and images of white women were also used in this particular article, readers are not likely to draw the same negative implicit ideas because there were many, many more varied images and articles of white women in that magazine. I have seen this same trend of using black people as examples for negative or embarrassing experiences also take place on talk shows.

Fiction books

When I was in high school, I read this fiction book which took place in a black Caribbean country with a black woman as the main character. This book actually dealt slightly with racism, showing the different experiences the two love interests had in the United States during the civil rights movement (one good, one bad). There was no problem with this story except the description of the main character's physical features. She was described in an order that went something like this: *Men looked appreciatively at her. She was pretty. She had straight hair, unlike the other girls in the town.* Since prettiness and having straight hair are put one after the other, the implicit message is that prettiness is equated with straight hair. So what made this black woman pretty was: she had straight hair unlike that of the other black women in the town.

Black women do not have straight hair; we have extremely curly or kinky hair (like the black women in that town). We may perm our hair to make it straight, but when new hair grows out of our scalps, it will be kinky. We may straighten our hair with a hot iron, but when we wash it, it will revert back to its natural kinky form. If having straight hair is what makes you pretty, then basically that description is implicitly saying all black women are ugly because no black woman (including that main character) naturally has straight hair. Another idea that will come as a result of this message is that if a black woman wants to be considered pretty then she must have non-black features either naturally or artificially. I don't believe the author of this book wrote this description to put black women down. Nevertheless, just because you never intended to hurt black people with your words or actions does not mean that you don't believe in an implicit racist idea that demeans black people, and that your resulting actions won't discriminate against and hurt black people.

Finally, I remember a children's story I read when I was younger. It was about a black doll that was mistreated because of his brown skin color by the other white dolls in the doll house. So this doll decided to run away and got caught in the rain. His running away caused the other dolls to repent of their bad behavior, and they decided to look for him, but to no avail. When this black doll returned to the house soaking wet, they apologized to him, but at the same time, his brown skin color began to come off because of the rain water, and he became white like the other dolls. This made all of them very happy because he was now white; the story ends. As a young reader, I felt happy for the black doll that he was now white. The implicit message sent here is that while it is wrong to mistreat black people, the skin color of white people is the best and that black people should aspire to be like Whites.

Advertisements

Living in Nigeria, I have been exposed to a lot of billboards and adverts on the road and in buses. What often strikes me as 'racially' insensitive is how a lot of these adverts use biracial or very light skinned models. I don't think there is anything wrong with using a biracial or light skinned model, after all there are Nigerians who are light skinned and biracial; However, the use of these types of models should be proportionate to the population. These very light skinned and biracial models do not represent the majority of the population where I live. So why are they frequently used? In Nigeria, one of the legacies of colonialism, which has also been continued by the media, is the belief that those who are light skinned are automatically beautiful. We even have billboards that advertise skin lightening products which are sold in supermarkets. Ironically, these skin lightening adverts sometimes use a biracial model. These Nigerian companies pick these models because they want their products to be modeled by people who are considered eye catching and beautiful. The implicit ideas these adverts send and reinforce to the Nigerian public is that light skinned and biracial women are prettier and more desirable than the average darker skinned Nigerian woman.

This is an example of colorism, and I have mentioned before that colorism is a result of racism. When I realized that God was not going to turn me into a white girl, I tried to become a light-skinned girl. I wanted to get my color as close to white as possible. I also wanted to marry a white man so that I could have light skinned biracial children who would be considered pretty and who wouldn't go through the same type of racism I was experiencing. Colorism can give non-Blacks the impression that they are not being racist because they are treating a black person properly (albeit a black person with a skin tone and features slightly similar to white people).

Film/television

I have watched movies and shows in which racism was falsely portrayed. For example, in one movie, a black maid was caught stealing and her white employer called the police on her. This movie portrayed the white employer as racist for calling the police. Calling the police when someone has stolen from you is not racist. It would have been racist if a white maid had done the same thing, but didn't face the same consequences. This false portrayal of racism sends the implicit idea that racism is really just *black people behaving badly, experiencing the consequences for their actions, and then crying racism*. This implicit idea delegitimizes black people's experiences with racism so that when they speak up about racist encounters, people refuse to believe them. They speculate 'what else happened' or 'what bad behavior' may have brought on the racist encounter. So they will say things like: "maybe that was just your perception", or "maybe you just misread the situation".

Another example of films and TV shows transmitting implicit racist ideas is a police drama that I used to watch in which I noticed a certain trend: when the victims of violence were black women, they were portrayed in a manner in which you felt no sympathy for them; and black characters, both men and women, were often portrayed as hardened and callous. As I watched their stories, I would feel disgust for these black characters. For example, there was an episode where a young black woman was beaten up by her black boyfriend in front of three witnesses; two of them were black, one was non-black. Only the non-black witness was willing to come forward and testify; the other two black characters refused to speak up. In another episode, a black athlete raped several women. While his black victims, portrayed as excessively materialistic, used the crimes committed against them as a means to greedily extort money from him (thereby making the viewers unsympathetic towards them), the white victim, on the other hand, was portrayed as truly traumatized (making viewers more sympathetic towards her).

Whenever the victims of violence were white women, they were portrayed in a manner in which you would sympathize with them. One of the police officers in the unit would fight both tooth and nail for them with compassion in her eyes, even when they did wrong things. The unit never seemed to react in the same charitable, compassionate manner when dealing with black victims. The majority of the black characters I have come across in this show were portrayed as unfeeling, hard, and cold hearted. These are the ideas the show is transmitting about black people, and when viewers see Blacks in this manner, *they* become hard, pitiless, and cold hearted towards Blacks. And they find it hard to see their cruel behavior because they operate under an implicit mindset that believes black people are unfeeling and unworthy of humane treatment.

Nowadays, in movies and TV shows that have black male characters (even in some music videos by black African artists), their love interests are almost always biracial, Latina, or white. In some rare cases, the woman will be fully black, but light-skinned. You find this even in movies with a majority black cast. Under realistic circumstances the majority of black male characters should be with a black female love interest, just like the majority of white male characters have white female love interests. In general, when a woman (or man) is the love interest of the protagonist in a movie (and in life), this person is put up on a pedestal because love cherishes and lifts people up. Some synonyms for the word cherish are: value, prize, and treasure. I have previously mentioned that there's a God-sized need in humans to be valued. So when movies and TV shows only put biracial (or light-skinned), Latina, and white women as the love interests of black men, they are sending out the message that these women are more valuable than black women and are to be more treasured and prized.

Even more alarming is when light-skinned or biracial actresses are chosen to portray inspiring real life dark skinned women with very African features. This act of exclusion sends the idea that nothing good has ever come out of dark-skinned black women, and that they are not worthy to be on screen. Moreover, these movies and TV shows have no problem putting dark-skinned black women in demeaning or negative roles so that people start to unconsciously view them in a bad light. You may be able to name one or two movies or TV shows where dark-skinned women are portrayed in a positive manner, but they are so few and far between that they don't really make a dent on the constant bombardment of negative images.

Furthermore, movies and TV shows put actors on a pedestal. Not just in terms of fame and success, but also in terms of beauty. There are some people who are out rightly beautiful. And there are some people who, if you spend time looking at their faces and bodies, you will eventually see their beauty, and this will also *normalize* their faces and bodies in your mind. When we watch TV, we are constantly watching the faces and bodies of actors. I have come to recognize and appreciate the beauty of plain looking non-black actresses because I have watched movies and TV shows they have acted in. When black and dark-skinned actresses are not given the roles that should go to them, or when they are just erased from stories that *are* about them, we never get the opportunity to see the different types of beauty found in black and dark-skinned women. Due to this, features that are specific to black and dark-skinned women, like our skin tones, facial structures, our lips, our noses, our butts, and our bodies remain outside of the repertoire of what is considered beautiful and normal. This implicitly teaches people, black women included, that our features are abnormal or an *Other*, and the effects of *othering* have been covered above. I believe that this is one of the reasons why I used to feel that a black woman and her body were out of place in a group of other non-black women.

Other brief examples

- A-list black women actresses are rarely given black men as love interests.
- Black men, especially young black men, are frequently portrayed as violent and criminal or being overtly big and strong.
- Black children on screen are often portrayed by biracial children.
- Black teenagers are often portrayed as the ones who mock the protagonist, especially in movies about high school.
- Black women in authority are frequently portrayed as an adversary, a villain, or an antagonist to the main character(s).
- Black people are at times not credited for trends they have started, but when this same trend is copied by a white person, the media portrays the white person as the one who created it or who is the best at it.
- Africa is often spoken of as a country instead of a continent, denying our individuality and diversity. Instead of saying, "I live in Nigeria", some people will say "I live in Africa", even though they have never lived in at least 3 of the 54 countries on the continent.

As you can see from these examples, none of them outrightly say that black people are inferior. Nevertheless, repetition of these negative images and behaviors ensures that implicit racist ideas will form. We get so used to seeing these images that they become the norm. When confronted with how these racist ideas are transmitted, some people might think "yeah, it's sad". They shrug their shoulders believing that the problem is out there, unaware that these images affect them unconsciously. Others become activists, also believing that the problem is also out there, but fail to recognize that they are just as vulnerable to being infected with these ideas. Others are aware of these racist beliefs in their minds, but have no clue how to deal with them, and so settle for feeling guilty.

*

In the next chapter, I will show you how I tackled racist ideas, thoughts, and beliefs in my life and how you can too.

7 LET THE BATTLE BEGIN

When I decided to tackle the anti-black racism in my life, I had no idea what I was doing. So looking back now, I can only credit God for these techniques that I used because they took the battle to where the battlefield was and effectively attacked the racist ideas in my mind.

The Journey

The tools I am going to give you in this chapter are not tools that you will only use once. You will need to use these tools every day because the battle against racism is a journey. Racist ideas that have been implicitly taught to us for years will have become strongholds in our minds, meaning that these ideas are like trees that have taken root. They won't go away in one day. It took more than a year before I saw some tangible results, and even then I still had a long way to go. Now, you may be thinking, "More than a year! That's too long of a time to remain a racist." However, please recall that I had allowed myself to become extremely brainwashed in regards to black people, I was only fourteen/fifteen years old, and it was not yet the age of smartphones through which I could have sped up the process. However, even though it took like forever in my young mind to see results, I just kept going, and I am glad I did. Being free of a racist mindset has been so rewarding.

If a random seed falls on fertile ground, it will grow into a plant whether or not you wanted that particular plant to grow. Therefore, you will also have to keep using these techniques as a shield because anti-black racist ideas are everywhere, and our minds are fertile grounds for thoughts and beliefs to spring up. So while you are uprooting racist beliefs, you are also preventing them from reforming.

As I have grown older and more knowledgeable, I have added some more techniques to my original ones. All these tools are ones that I have applied and continue to apply. Some of them have become a natural part of my life, and I do them without thinking. I cannot say that these are the only tools available. If you realize that you have been applying other techniques that have been effective, then please continue to do so as you apply these new ones. Also, some of these techniques may not be applicable to everyone as you may not have struggled with the same implicit racist ideas, so in those specific cases, take the idea behind the technique and apply it to the areas where you struggle.

These tools may seem simple and 'old news' to some, but just because something is simple does not mean people will do it. People are often looking for complex and new sounding solutions to fix their problems instead of doing the simple things they were taught by their parents and some teachers. Nevertheless, putting these techniques into practice was not easy for me.

No more guilt or shame

As I tackled racism in my life, I eventually realized that I had been brainwashed. This knowledge helped to remove the guilt and shame I felt about my racist thoughts and beliefs because I realized that racism did not come from me. As you tackle racism in your life, first recognize that you were taught to be racist. Second, understand that you cannot prevent a thought from entering your head; all you can do is to refuse to accept it and stop yourself from constantly thinking about it or dwelling on it. With this in mind, do not condemn yourself or feel shame for racist thoughts and beliefs in your mind. God does not condemn you, so do not condemn yourself; it is counterproductive. If you realize that you have given in to a racist thought or that you discriminated against a black person, do not get defensive, admit you were wrong, remember you were taught to be racist, and make up your mind to do better next time. Like I said before, this is a journey; it might not be easy for some people to break free from beliefs that have been deeply rooted in their minds, but just have faith that it will get better even if you do not see instant results, and don't give up. It got better for me because I kept going.

The Techniques

1.Pay attention and call it out

In the previous chapter I gave a few examples of how racist ideas get passed. So when battling racism in your life, one of the first things we need to do is to pay attention to these areas and other areas you can find. Start to watch out for repetitions in the ways black people are portrayed in magazines, books, on the news, and on screen. If you read history books that only tell you about white history, ask yourself what were black people (and other groups of people) also doing around that time. Pay attention to how black people are treated in schools, malls, supermarkets, and in other places. Work out why what you notice is racist and call it out in your mind. Implicit racism will lose its cover of darkness now that you are aware of it and are calling it out.

Many months ago, I was leaving a crowded mall in Nigeria when I noticed a dark skinned, big chested, and dreadlocked hair man coming into the mall at the same time. I was many meters away from him, but in a split second, I felt this man was dangerous, and I made up my mind to walk a wide berth away from him. A second later, I realized that I was projecting danger onto this man because he was dark, his chest was big (he wasn't even tall), and because his hair was in dreadlocks. I knew I was wrong, that I was discriminating, but I was still slightly fearful of moving close to this man, so I remained immobile. Eventually, he passed me, oblivious of me, and oblivious that I had just had a racist, prejudiced view of him. I understand that God can warn us of people and things by giving us certain emotions about them, but I knew that all those fearful thoughts had nothing to do with God. They were irrational; they were based on the fact that the man was dark and had a big chest (remember The big black man syndrome). I asked myself how this fear had slipped into my mind. I was not surrounded by a people or culture that broadcasted these ideas of black men. The only other viable entry point was what I had been watching, and yes, I had been watching shows, movies, and news programs that broadcasted ideas of black men being dangerous. I believe that I exposed myself to these implicit ideas for quite some time, and I also did not call it out, so it was able to slip in and plant roots.

To fight against implicit racism, there will be some things that you will have to turn off or avoid because they will only hinder your journey. However, this is a personal decision you must make for yourself. There are some movies that I do not watch because I have noticed that after I finish watching them, I feel like I have to defend my worth as a black woman.

2. Refuse to accepts racist thoughts

When I started my anti-racism journey, I made the decision to reject anti-black racist thoughts that came into my mind. How I did this was by saying, "I don't believe that", when a negative thought would come. These thoughts kept coming of course, and even my feelings would say that I did believe them; but I just kept saying to myself, "I don't believe that". With time, these negative thoughts about black people came less frequently, and I truly began to disbelieve them. My feelings also aligned with my beliefs. Today, I am free from the explicit negative beliefs I had about black people. I don't view black men and women in the same negative manner I used to. I see us as individuals. Some explicit racist thoughts do come from time to time, but my mind is already prepared to battle them using this technique and other techniques I have learnt. They don't stay long because I give them quite a thrashing.

3. Look at black people

In order to change my beliefs of Blacks being generally ugly and unattractive, I decided to spend time looking at pictures of black people. My aim was to find at least one pretty thing about them. So, whenever I flipped through magazines, I would stop and look at pictures of black men and women. Since I generally ignored pictures of black people, I would often flip the page before I realized that there was an image of a black person on the previous page, and then I would make myself go back to look at the picture. I would spend a few seconds just looking at the black person. This was not easy for me because of how brainwashed I had become. In my mind, I could not see a future in which I would find black people attractive. I did not immediately find something pretty, much less beautiful, but I just kept looking at images. Eventually, I would see something that I considered a little pretty, and I would say it to myself. "Oh, she has pretty eyes".

Why this worked and works is because of what I mentioned in the previous chapter about how I have come to appreciate the beauty of non-black actresses by watching movies they act in. When you spend time looking at someone, eventually you will see their beauty because everyone is truly beautiful in their own way. That is really not a cliché. Furthermore, doing this makes you familiar with black features, making them less abnormal to you.

After what seemed like a long time of doing this (over a year; I was around sixteen/seventeen years old), one day, as I was walking around, a wall in my mind just broke down, and I realized that black men were actually quite handsome. Unfortunately, I decided that this breakthrough was enough, that I no longer needed to apply this technique. In hindsight, I see that I was not completely free of a racist mindset in this area because I was still determined to marry a white man (the young rapper I previously had a crush on had been replaced by older white actors), but I gave myself a pat on the back for considering black men as handsome. Don't get me wrong, I am not saying that you should not want to marry a white man or woman or that you have to marry a black man or woman in order for you to fight racism in your life. I also understand that some people just have an innate preference for white, Asian, black, tall, or short men and women that has nothing to do with being brainwashed. What I am saying is that *my motive* for wanting to marry a white man was still racist – meaning I just saw white men as having more value than black men though I did not actually value them for who they were. What I valued was the beauty and status white superiority racist ideas had painted for me.

What helped refresh my lagging journey was the realization that I had been brainwashed. This realization came about when memories of my life before the brainwashing resurfaced. I remembered that I actually used to view black guys as attractive, and that I had never actually looked at white guys before. I realized that that my desire for white men actually was not my own, neither was the belief that white beauty was superior to black beauty. These were instead other people's racist beliefs that I had accepted as the truth, suppressing my own innate ideas. I started looking at black people again. Today, I find black men to be handsome, good looking, attractive, and desirable. I love their different shades of brown, and I would like to marry a black man by God's grace. I see them as individual men who can be gentle and romantic. I also find black women, dark-skinned and light-skinned, to be pretty, beautiful, gorgeous, and attractive. I subscribe to Facebook pages that are devoted to posting up pictures of black women. I love our features such as our hair, our lips, and our butts (thanks to Beyonce's Bootylicious song). In addition, the beauty or attractiveness I now see in white men is their own innate beauty, not the one racism brainwashed me with.

Nevertheless, I am not condemning anyone for their desires, whether their motives are pure or not so pure. If you want to marry a non-black or black person for whatever reason, I say, "Go ahead". I did not get to where I am now in a few months or a year or two. It has taken years, and honestly, I have not yet arrived. My journey has been in stages, and sometimes when I have had a breakthrough, I would stop fighting and rest on my laurels. I am just glad that I started this journey.

4. Speak well about black people

Another technique that I employed was that whenever I saw images of black women in magazines and on TV, I would make myself say out loud, "she's pretty", if I saw a little something that was pretty in them. I did this to strengthen the feeble idea of black women's beauty in my mind. My sister, who did not know the mind battle that was going on, wondered why I called almost every black woman I saw pretty. "You don't have to say that every time you see a black woman", she would say. I think my sister sensed that my words were not genuinely felt, that it was like a compulsion for me to say them. Nevertheless, as I have grown older, I have come to recognize the power in words. I have learnt that just like ideas, our words can also form our thoughts, beliefs, and actions. We can change our lives by changing the things we say. Proverbs 18:2[1], a verse in the Bible says: "Life and death are in the power of the tongue, and those who love it will eat its fruit". Basically, this verse says that our words are like seeds which have the power to produce a harvest of good things (life) or bad things (death). By calling black women pretty even when I barely believed it, I was planting the seeds that would help me truly see our beauty and attractiveness. I applied this same technique on myself because for a long time I saw myself as unattractive. Everyday, I would recite bible verses that spoke about beauty over myself. I did this for some time until I got busy with other things and forgot to say it. Many months later, I realized that I no longer saw myself as unattractive, and I actually began to see some prettiness in myself. I knew that it was those words that had brought about the change. As you can imagine, I quickly went back to calling myself beautiful. So if there is a negative opinion you have of black people, start saying a positive thing that negates that negative view. And you do not have to say it in front of others until you genuinely believe it.

5. Black love and stories

When I see movies and TV shows that almost always put the main black male character with a non-black female love interest, or the main black female character with a non-black male love interest, I am reminded of how I used to feel uncomfortable when I saw two black people kissing on screen. Yet, I could watch two white people kissing thinking how romantic it was. I made the decision to start watching black couples being romantic on screen. What this does is that as you see black people cherishing each other in romantic situations, black people become less and less of an Other in your mind. It humanizes black people. You will start to see them as you see yourself. Today, I enjoy watching black romance movies.

I also make an effort to seek out stories written by black writers with mainly black characters in movies, TV shows, and books. When I was younger, what I had access to were fictional stories with mainly white characters. Now that I am older, I make an effort to also read stories with mainly black characters. Aside from humanizing people, reading diverse fictional stories about black people helps to fight against stereotypes in our minds.

6. Get some knowledge and cultural exposure

As my anti-racism journey progressed, I decided to learn more about African history because I saw that it was important in countering negative ideas about black people. Lies thrive on ignorance. When you do not know something, people can easily shape how you think of that thing. So I checked out historical fiction books about African kingdoms, like books about Nzinga, the ancient queen of present day Angola. I have read stories about the innovative history of African Americans. And I am currently working on finding out more about pre-colonial African history for a fantasy book I want to write.

Another technique is to get some cultural exposure. Go online and find out about the different tourist sites in African countries and in black nations to help you broaden your knowledge and the images you have of black people, even if you do not want to visit these areas. Learn about the different types of culinary dishes made by African Americans, Africans, and in the Caribbean. Find out about Ethiopia's centuries old Christian heritage. Listen to some African music on YouTube; and if you have the opportunity, learn your African or black language. This will increase your respect of black people and culture and combat the negative images of them.

7. Religion

As I have grown older and learnt more things about the Bible, I make an effort to view Jesus as black in my mind. I personally don't believe that Jesus' skin color is white or black. He is God; He created humans with the ability to have different colors and features, so He certainly is not confined to one color or feature. I have heard stories about people who have had visions of Jesus, and their descriptions of Him vary. One person said He had brown hair and green eyes, another person said He had blond hair and blue eyes, and another person said that when he went to Malaysia, the Jesus in His dreams looked like a Malaysian. When Jesus was on earth He would grant people things saying: "According to your faith let it be done to you"[2] (Matthew 9:29, Matthew 8:13). Meaning however you want it to happen, let it happen like that. So I believe that the color you picture Him in your mind is how He will appear to you.

Furthermore, there was a man in the Bible called Job, who lamented that God could not understand him because God was not like him (Job 9:32). So Jesus was sent to earth as a human being. There are verses in the Bible that stress Jesus' humanity and stress that He understands our emotions, struggles, and temptations because He too was human (Hebrews 4:15). Therefore, I can say that even the Bible recognizes the human need to know that God is like you. The African nations that were evangelized were given a packaged Gospel of Jesus and other religious figures as white. It is time for Africans to unpack this image of Jesus and other religious figures, and to repack them as black for African audiences.

8. Play the underdog's advocate

During my brainwashed stage, whenever I saw a black person either in real life or on TV in a tight situation, the thoughts that came into my mind would blame that black person for that situation. I never wanted to condemn the black person because condemning them felt like I was condemning myself, but I could not seem to help those thoughts. Black people get criticized harsher than their white counterparts for wrong behavior because people are not just condemning the action, they are also condemning the blackness in the person. I believe that black people's mistakes (sometimes real and sometimes imagined) are the avenues people use to release their pent up anti-blackness. What I mean is that when people criticize Blacks, anti-blackness piggybacks on these criticisms. Even studies show that black people in the USA have gotten higher sentences for the same crimes that their white counterparts have committed[3].

So when I began my journey to fight anti-black racism in my mind, I decided to play the underdog's advocate. Whenever I came across a situation in which a black person was condemned or just portrayed in a negative light, I would pause and not be so quick to condemn the black person or to immediately assume that they were at fault as in previous times. I am not talking about justifying criminal and mean behavior, no, I am talking about asking myself if there really was a legitimate reason to find fault with the black person in question. For example, I would put myself in the shoes of unarmed black men, women, and kids who were killed by police officers in the United States. I would empathize with black people who had suffered a tragedy instead of looking for reasons to blame them for their pain. I would not accept the label of black women on reality shows as being aggressive. I would refuse to just go along with the negative portrayal of black female antagonists in fiction stories. Instead I look for reasons to understand their supposed negative actions in these tales because I began to sense that black female characters were being used as scapegoats.

I found that when I did this, I would sometimes find that there was no basis to dislike or reprimand some black people and characters. It also helped me fight against the racist mentality that sought to condemn black people and sought to hold them up to a standard that no one could keep or was keeping. Once again, I want to stress that this technique is not about justifying the wrong actions of some black people.

9. Question whether your perception is accurate

This next technique is similar to the previous one. Racist ideas and the resulting prejudices twist things in our minds to the extent that even what we see becomes distorted, or we convince ourselves that we are seeing certain things even though they do not exist. For me, this explains why I could buy many things at a store frequently, yet the workers in the store would keep treating me like I was a thief who was looking to steal their merchandise. It also explains why some teachers graded some of my assignments like they were of little value, even though on those occasions my classmates and I knew that the quality of my work was high. I was just seen as not capable of producing high quality work. And it explains why I was called aggressive in certain areas even though there was no logical proof that I was a forceful person. These people had an image of Blacks in their minds and convinced themselves that they were seeing that image in me. They interpreted my behavior and work according to the prejudice in their minds.

Therefore, one tool that I use to discern racism in my life is to evaluate whether the perception I have of a black person is accurate or based on racial prejudice. I give reasons to justify my beliefs about a person, and I make sure I have proof. However, you need to give your evaluation some time because implicit racist ideas are not jumping around our heads saying "I'm right here! Can you see me?" You have to keep a watchful eye over your thoughts and perceptions about certain black people over a period of time before you can truly know if your perceptions are based on implicit racism. For example, for a period of time, I disliked a particular black woman on a TV show, and I thought I had a valid reason for why I did not like her, but I didn't really evaluate it in my mind. After some time, I became conscious that the reason for my dislike was not valid or logical. When I finally admitted this to myself, I was able to discern that the reason I disliked this black woman was because she was black and innocently confident. I realized that I was jealous of her because though she was black like me, she had an unconscious confidence that I no longer had, that I had given away when I decided to believe the racist ideas about myself and black people.

Another thing that can help you recognize whether your perception is real or just prejudice is to look for positive things about that black person. Some of the positive things you find might actually negate the negative perception you have. Be open to change if you find that your beliefs are prejudiced.

10. 'If it was a white person' test

This next technique is also slightly similar to the previous one. When I found out I was black, I did not have a good definition of racism. I thought racism meant that you hated all black people and treated all of them badly. This limited definition prevented me from identifying racism against myself. For example, not all my black schoolmates were mistreated as I was by some teachers, so I discarded the notion that these specific teachers were mistreating me because of the color of my skin. Once again, I want to point out that the mistreatment I am talking about **is not** teachers reprimanding me for my misdeeds. I am referring to things that were said and done to me and beliefs that were projected on me that had no basis.

It was during my university days that I was exposed to more knowledge about racism. This new knowledge pointed out to me that my previous experiences were inspired by racism. I was very reluctant to believe this because I could not reconcile why some black schoolmates were not mistreated as I was. Yet, there was an insistence in my mind to consider this. Then a question came up within me that said: forget about how other black people were treated, just ask yourself this question: "If you had been white, would they have treated you in this manner?" The moment I heard this question, I knew the answer: No. White and non-black kids in the schools I went to were treated much better than black kids, even when they were punished. They were viewed as smarter, treated with exclusive familiarity, and some of their misbehavior ignored. There was no doubt in my mind that had I been white, I would have been treated much better and gotten better grades. I had to accept that some of the treatment I experienced at the hands of certain teachers was due to the color of my skin; it was racist.

As my knowledge of racism grew, I came to understand how other factors like poverty, being rich, beauty, fame, friendships, and behavior can along with racism influence how you are treated. Some factors can protect you up to a certain point from racism, and some factors can make you an easy target to experience racism. For example, in some cases, a rich black person will get treated better than a poor black person. Other times, some people who are quiet and not so open with their personality close a lot of inroads that people may try to use to mistreat them. I realized that some of my black schoolmates had other factors working for them that protected them to an extent from racism. If I had been white, my lack of 'other factors' would not have mattered, I would still have been treated better.

So one method I use to check racism in my life is to ask myself these questions when I am in certain situations: *"If this person was white, would I treat them/feel this way?", "If this person was black, would I treat them/feel this way?", and "Has any white person done the same thing, and how did I respond to them?"* Since it was predominantly white history that I was taught, predominantly white actors that I watched, predominantly white films that get the most publicity and that are nominated in award shows that get talked about on international news media, and predominantly white stories that I have read, white people have been presented to me with a human face. This humanization makes me prone to care more for white people, to empathize and sympathize more with them, to be more interested in them and their stories, and to treat white people better. On the other hand, black people's histories are relatively unknown and purported to not exist, our stories and our films (and those of other ethnicities) do not receive as much publicity, some of our actresses are excluded on screen, and we are often portrayed with a negative and sometimes evil face, relegated to needing a white savior. On top of that, we have been conditioned to mistreat black people, to deny them their rights, and to dehumanize them. In short, people find it hard to see black people with a human face; therefore it takes extra effort to care about them, to sympathize and empathize with them, and to be interested in their stories. By asking myself these questions, I try to figure out if I have been giving Whites and Non-Blacks undeserved privilege and if I am treating black people properly.

11. Stop survivor blaming

During my school days, I could sometimes get a sense whether a teacher would like or dislike me. Therefore, I was extremely cautious in my behavior around those teachers in order to protect myself from being mistreated. I did not want to give them any reason to justify their prejudice. Although this sometimes shielded me, a lot of times it didn't work; I would still get treated in a prejudiced manner. Unfortunately, there are people who take the idea behind my actions to an extreme. They believe black people can stop racism against themselves by being perfect in all situations. And what they mean by perfect is based on whether or not the black person in question was mistreated, meaning if you were discriminated against, then your behavior was not perfect. They imply that black people must have done something wrong to be badly treated or that they deserve discrimination because of their misbehavior (real or imagined). They do not hold the person who behaved in a racist manner accountable for their own behavior. This particular stance is untrue and unjust because it disregards racism and the fact that everyone has control over their own actions.

Blacks have grown up hearing that they have to behave better and work ten times harder than others in order to get what is rightfully theirs. I will not dissuade anybody from going this extra mile. If you have to work harder, be less open with people, or be extremely careful in certain situations, then do all these things, *when you can*. I say this because there is some wisdom in doing these things even if racism was not involved. However, remember that going the extra mile will not always protect you. Also, keep in mind…..

- The expectation that black people have to be perfect or work harder in order not to suffer racism is **wrong.** People of other 'races' do not have to do this, so why should black people?

- Trying to always be perfect in order to avoid discrimination will only leave black people frustrated, stressed out, and angry.

- Black people will sometimes make mistakes because they are human like everyone else.

- Black people who do wrong things should be punished according to their misdeed, not according to the racism inside of people.

- The person who behaves in a racist manner is responsible for his/her own actions and cannot use the misdeeds (real or imagined) of a black person to justify their racist behavior.

- Anti-black racism is like an abusive and domineering person who wants to hold all the cards in a relationship and make and change the rules as they go. Today, it expects black people to be silent; tomorrow, it accuses Blacks of not speaking up; the next day, it berates Blacks for talking too much. No matter what black people do, it will always find fault.

When we do not recognize these points listed above, we start to blame black people (ourselves) because we feel they (we) did not work hard enough. We forget that it is *an extra mile*, that there are other people who are not going this extra mile and are not being mistreated. We do not recognize that by expecting black people to always go the extra mile, we are holding them (ourselves) up to a standard that nobody can keep. Black people are human beings like the rest; we are not perfect, and our imperfections are no different from others. Black children are no different from white and non-black children. Children of all 'races' can be disorganized, loud, thoughtless, and rowdy. Teenagers of all colors go through phases where some can be irresponsible, unwilling to work, disorganized, and hormonal. Why do we demand that black children behave like adults if they do not want to be mistreated (even killed)? Why do we deny them their rights to a childhood and growth phases? Why do we expect black men and women to always be well spoken, without emotion, and without resistance even in the face of injustice when others would never respond like this? Going the extra mile is done to survive, but human beings are not meant to be living in survival mode. It should not be normalized in our minds because it is not normal. I keep these thoughts in mind so that I do not start blaming black people for the injustices they suffer.

12. Avoid the poverty trap

Poor people are sometimes despised, looked down upon, patronized, and discriminated against. As humans, we generally like those who can give us something, whether it is knowledge, money, fame, status, or power. People who live in poverty can't offer much, if anything at all. Some of them are needy and not as 'refined' as people of greater financial means. All of this tends to repel people. Not only so, human beings sometimes see poor people as props, meaning we help poor people not necessarily because we care about them, but because we want the world and our conscience to see that we are good people.

African countries are not as developed as western countries and experience problems that are easily taken care of in developed nations. A lot of black people and countries are linked to poverty. Even though there are of course many rich and middle class black people, unfortunately the 'single story' that is constantly broadcasted is the image of poor black people. Furthermore, the hundreds of years of wars, ethnic and religious clashes, diseases, poverty, corruption, and nation building that western countries experienced before they arrived at their 'developed' status are not frequently considered in the development narrative to give people perspective. The contributions of slavery and colonization to these western nations' economies are also not frequently broadcasted. What this does is that it gives people the opinion that western (and majority white) countries developed overnight through their own labor, power, intelligence, and money. This opinion can lead people to think that there is something wrong with black African countries (and therefore black people) who are still struggling to develop.

I have previously spoken about how anti-black racism piggy-backs on other issues- poverty being one of them. Poor Blacks are especially despised, condemned, and patronized. Therefore, one technique that I use to fight against implicit racism is to repeatedly tell myself to be understanding of people who are not as financially well off as I am, to not judge them for the position they are in, and to not fantasize about being a financial or emotional 'savior' to them. Doing all this closes inroads through which implicit racism can be expressed.

Another technique that I have learnt is not to take sole credit for my position in life or my accomplishments, but instead to thank God for the things that I have. This might seem unfair to some people who feel like they should get credit for the efforts they have put in, after all the merits of working hard have been preached to us from a young age. While I am not dissuading the importance of hard work or denying the role it plays in our success, I have learnt that not everything is due to hard work. There are many other factors that play a role in our successes that we have no control over. For example, it was not by our hard work that we are alive today (how successful can a corpse be?). Neither was it by our hard work that we were born into families/nations that paid for our education; how successful can we truly be if we can't read or write? We do not know where our effort stops and where the grace of God and factors we have no control over begin. We do not know who else worked even harder than us, yet due to certain circumstances are not as successful as us. It is a human weakness to feel superior to those who are in positions lower than us, especially poor people. We like to think that we worked harder than them to get to where we are, and that if they had just worked as hard, they would not be in the low position they are in. This is a perfect atmosphere for racism to enter and thrive, and the best way to combat this is by making the decision to just thank God and to be grateful for what we have in life.

13. Choose to value black lives

One way to fight against racism is by choosing to value black lives. Since white people are portrayed as the standard for humanity in terms of beauty, history, and culture in many societies, their lives are valued more. On the other hand, black lives are perceived as being of lower value. So, in order to combat this ridiculous perception, I make an effort to value things that come from black people, whether it is their opinions, their cultures, their art forms, and their men and women. I make an effort to not automatically dismiss things that are said or done by black people. I repeatedly tell myself that black people are interesting, and I make an effort to look at black people's photos on Facebook, watch our vlogs on YouTube, and listen to news about black celebrities. I deliberately watch black award shows and view them in my mind with the same prestige as I would view the Oscars. I make an effort to watch black TV dramas and predominantly black movies. I empathize with black characters, and I constantly remind myself to pray for black celebrities and black people on the news like I do for white ones. I choose to be horrified, enraged, and saddened by tragedies that happen to black people worldwide, not just when tragedies happen to white people. In short, I do things that help me to value black lives, culture, and history, to put us on a pedestal like white people have been put.

14. Avoid the Colorism trap

When I started practicing the technique of looking at black people in magazines, I found myself gravitating more towards pictures of lighter-skinned and biracial black (LSBB) men. I spent less time looking at the darker skinned black (DSB) men in favor of the lighter skinned ones. I justified myself saying that "they're after all black". After doing this for awhile, I felt God speak to my heart that I was not really changing or accomplishing anything. I had to be honest with myself and acknowledge that I was appreciating these LSBB men only because of their closeness in skin tone to white people. I made the decision then to not spend time looking at LSBB men in magazines or movies. I saw that the racism I was fighting against had no problems with LSBB men. So I began to spend more time looking at DSB men and women, not only in magazines but also on the street.

Colorism values anything that is close to white; it is basically a form of white privilege given to non-white people. Here are some techniques I currently use to fight against colorism in my life: When I am among black people, the unconscious tendency is for my eyes to be drawn to those who are lighter skinned or to give them a second glance because there is an implicit idea that LSBB people are more attractive. So in situations like these, I stop myself from giving that extra glance. But if I fall into that trap, I counter it by giving DSB people a second glance as well. I also repeatedly reject the thought that it is harder to see the features of darker skinned people. What all this does is that I am repeatedly making my mind put LSBB and DSB on the same level.

Now I am not saying that the beauty of LSBB should not be appreciated or that their skin tone should not be admired. The skin tone of LSBB *should* be appreciated, but not because it is closer to white and therefore pretty, but because it has *always* been pretty regardless of its closeness to white. For example, I love how black eyebrows, eyelashes, and hair, contrast with light brown skin. I also love the light skin tones of African American rapper Eve and African American actress Sanaa Lathan. There is something so beautiful about their skin tones, and I know in my heart that the beauty I see in their colors is a beauty that I have found, not a beauty that colorism brainwashed me to believe.

I have to make an effort to be honest with myself in this area because it is not always easy to admit that I have been operating under a colorism mindset, especially when you think you are past all that. An example of this is a few years back, I came across a biracial light skinned man, and my teenage hormones got resurrected as I began to obsess about this guy, surfing the internet for anything I could find on him since he was a celebrity. In the thick of this hormonal behavior, I warily began to wonder whether I was crushing on this guy because I really found him attractive or because he was biracial and light skinned. So, I decided to really search my heart; it took some time for me to find the truth. I believe that I was interested in him as a celebrity because he was biracial, but I was interested in him physically because he was very tall and slightly muscular, features that I am very attracted to. Nowadays, I make an effort not to give LSBB celebrities more attention than I do DSB celebrities. If I find that I have fallen into that trap, I deliberately counter it by also giving the same attention to DSB celebrities.

Another point that needs to be mentioned is that masculinity has been linked with dark colors. Consequently, a lot of people with dark features and skin tones, especially black men, are viewed as more masculine. Furthermore, DSB men are viewed as more masculine than LSBB men. This idea has even been accepted by some black people, and I used to subscribe to it myself. I think this is because there are a lot of negative ideas out there about black men, so when a seemingly positive idea is broadcasted, it tends to be easily accepted by some black people. However, I chose to stop viewing DSB men as more masculine after reading a comment online in which the person commenting basically said that if people were going to hold on to this idea, then they shouldn't get upset if LSBB women were also viewed as more feminine than DSB women. Unfortunately, black women have also been linked to masculinity. One technique that I currently employ is that whenever I describe black women, especially DSB women, one adjective that I repeatedly use is the word feminine.

In conclusion, do not fall into the trap of thinking, 'I'm black; I don't need to fight against colorism'. Let me just remind you that the racism I experienced in my life did not always come from non-black people but from people with black ancestry who had internalized anti-black racist ideas. Finally, I am also black, and I still have to be vigilant against colorism.

These techniques have helped me and continue to help me in my fight against implicit racism in my mind. Being set free from a racist mindset has been so rewarding. It has liberated me and continues to set me free from shame and a sense of inferiority. This freedom has made me more understanding of people who also operate with an implicit racist mindset because I know how their beliefs were formed and what it takes to uproot these beliefs. It has also helped me appreciate people of different colors for who they are, not for the color of their skin. It is a journey I would recommend everyone to take.

*

In the next chapter, I will touch on one more technique, which I feel carries great importance in the fight against implicit racism.

8 THE RISE OF THE INDIVIDUAL

I want to address how colorism sometimes affects the relationships between some light skinned Blacks, biracial Blacks, and dark skinned Blacks (DSB). The fact is that many societies, including black ones, place light skinned and biracial Blacks (LSBB) on a higher level than DSB, who are often mistreated. I believe this phenomenon leads to feelings of superiority and entitlement among some LSBB, but hurt, anger, bitterness, jealousy, and distrust among some DSB. The hurt and anger some DSB may feel come because of the discrimination they have faced. I believe bitterness comes because black people of all shades are already excluded in many areas, so when LSBB get a little privilege, some DSB feel even more excluded and jealous. Moreover, resentment and distrust build when some LSBB, who are shielded from some discrimination, fail to understand their privilege and the different levels of discrimination DSB face. Some indirectly blame DSB by brushing aside the racism in the situation and saying that DSB should just work harder and behave better. I have noticed that it is sometimes hard for people to understand and empathize with others who have faced higher levels of discrimination than they have. Furthermore, some DSB deal with all these emotions (which do not necessarily operate at the same time) by mistreating LSBB, which in turn reproduces similar feelings of hurt, anger, and resentment in some LSBB now directed at DSB.

Another issue in the same category is the biracial (and mixed 'race') quest for an identity that is separate from black people. I personally believe in embracing one's full ethnic makeup whether you are mixed 'race' or of mixed ethnicities, and I do not believe Biracials should have to identify as black (or should be accused of not being 'black enough'). I have heard some Biracials identify as mixed, and I get a sense that they are truly embracing their experience and ethnic makeup. However, there are other times when I have encountered some Biracials who strongly state that they should not be called black, and in these particular cases, I get a sense of anti-blackness. It seems to me that they blame black people for being called black or that all black people expect Biracials to identify as black (though some do). In addition, there is also this idea that black people are 'claiming' Biracials since 'Blacks don't have any people of value amongst themselves' because in some people's minds, anyone that has some connection to white is more valuable than anyone entirely black. In my opinion, I sense that this anti-blackness stems from a desire to avoid the prejudice and discrimination that black people face.

In the following paragraphs, I will discuss how DSB, LSBB, and Biracials can individually deal with the effects of colorism.

Dismantling white privilege

The technique that I have used to combat these issues mentioned above is to realize that the source of all our contention is white privilege, and that my focus should be on dismantling it. Synonyms of the word privilege are: benefit, advantage, opportunity, freedom, and right. In many cases, white people are automatically given some of these things because of the color of their skin. This does not mean that white people do not face struggles and some discrimination in life like everybody else. While white people do experience difficulties in life, there are many benefits they receive solely because of the color of their skin. Benefits that people of other colors are not automatically given. Another way to explain privilege is to look at how rich people are treated in comparison to poor people. Rich and poor people of all colors all experience difficult times, yet rich people are generally treated with more respect, given the benefit of the doubt, and receive more leniency because this world values money. White privilege has created a system of inequality where one group *is easily given* unearned benefits and readily given their earned ones. I want to clearly state that dismantling white privilege is not about attacking or lecturing white people, it is once again about combating white privilege ideas and beliefs in your mind; and in the coming paragraphs, I will share the techniques I use to accomplish that.

LSBB are sometimes given some of the benefits of white privilege because they have a semblance to whiteness. However, LSBB and DSB need to always keep in mind that the privileges LSBB get are often crumbs compared to the thousands of slices of cake that white people get. LSBB also experience racism because of their blackness. Therefore, there is no need for LSBB to feel superior or DSB to feel jealous, bitter, and suspicious over *crumbs*. Anything that causes Blacks to fight among ourselves is a distraction from dealing with racism within us and in the world because it makes us forget about the source of our contention: white privilege.

Focusing entirely on white privilege will help DSB to keep feelings of jealousy, bitterness, and distrust at bay. One crucial technique is to not question the 'blackness' or rather the belongingness of LSBB among other

Blacks no matter how they look or behave. Questioning the 'blackness' of a person unconsciously buys into the stereotype that all black people look or behave the same way, which is not true. Now, I want to clearly state that this does not mean that we should not point out cases of colorism. For example, when certain LSBB actresses are offered roles in Hollywood that should rightfully and historically go to a DSB actress, we should speak out against the *system* that seeks to 'whitewash' true life DSB figures and refuses to give opportunities to both DSB and LSBB actresses that rightfully belong to them. If we focus on condemning these actresses for taking such roles, it gets painted as a fight amongst black people, and those upholding the system of white privilege can easily slink away. No one remembers that they were the chess players and that the LSBB actresses were just their willing pawns. Blacks who have mistreated and vilified DSB should be viewed in the same light- *willing pawns* in the hands of a system that seeks to put black people down. It is therefore crucial that we keep our focus entirely on attacking the root of the problem, which is the system of white privilege. I have to repeatedly remind myself to focus on this, and I also remind myself that there are many LSBB who are actively fighting against colorism.

Following the twelfth technique in chapter seven can help LSBB fight against feelings of superiority that may try to creep in. It is always much wiser to thank God for the things that you have than to credit yourself for your position in life. Doing this can alleviate the feelings of guilt that some LSBB may feel when it is pointed out that they receive some unearned privileges. Another technique is to refuse to accept (in your mind) any praise that directly or indirectly states that your light skin tone is superior to darker skin tones. Constantly remind yourself that your light skin is beautiful because God made it beautiful, not because it is close to white. Finally, recognize that those DSB who have mistreated LSBB were also willing pawns of the system of white privilege.

One way Biracials (and those who are mixed 'race') can prevent feelings of anti-blackness from hijacking the expression of their mixed identity is to refuse to accept (in your mind) any praise that directly or indirectly states that you are superior to Blacks. Also, be careful that your need to be called biracial does not stem from the desire to be treated better than black people. This desire is a trap because instead of fighting against the system of white privilege, it tries to make a niche for itself within the system. It indirectly agrees with the system that black people (and ironically biracial Blacks) are inferior and should be mistreated, and that white people are superior and should be given unearned privileges. Constantly remind yourself that you should not experience racism and discrimination because you are a human being, not because you are half white or half non-black. Everyone should be treated well because they are human beings, not because of the color of their skin or how many non-black parents they have. Finally, recognize that it is the system of white privilege that decides who gets treated properly and how much, not black people.

The rise of the individual

Finally, a great way I fight against white privilege is to constantly make an effort to see black people (and all people for that matter) as individuals. This is not the so called 'colorblind' approach that claims to treat everyone equally, but refuses to acknowledge color patterns of discrimination. The common colorblind approach is dependent on the goodness of people's hearts; it basically states that "Because I am a good person and my parents taught me well, I will treat everyone equally regardless of their color." Yet throughout this book, I have shown that racism enters people through implicit ideas, and that no matter how well meaning you are, if you do not actively protect your mind, racist ideas will still affect you.

The technique that helps me see people as individuals is to not stereotype or make blanket statements about groups of people, even if it is a positive stereotype. Not stereotyping people is considered the political correct thing to say, but deep down I used to believe that different 'races', including black people, shared certain behavioral traits. Fortunately, the longer I have lived and the different people I have been exposed to have all led me to conclude that people of the same color, country, and ethnicity are not all the same. While some black people (and others) might have some similarities because they come from the same culture, there are many other factors that have nothing to do with culture like religious beliefs, income, society, experience, the media, and your choices that can all play a role in a person's behavior. Also, all black people do not share the same culture, even those who come from the same country. Furthermore, no one has ever met each and every single person in this world, so we cannot use the small sample of people we have come into contact with to conclude that most people from a particular ethnicity are like this or like that. Besides, we sometimes ignore the people who have behaved differently in a particular 'race' and only focus on those who have behaved the same to justify the stereotypes in our minds.

The black identity

Another important thing that needs to be addressed when fighting against white privilege is the so called 'black identity' and 'black community'. One very big privilege white people receive is that of being viewed as individuals while black people and people of other colors are viewed as a group or a community. I once watched a program in which a non-black American woman sincerely spoke about how she tried not to see black men as dangerous, but the fact was that the majority of crimes committed in her community were by black men. The logic this woman was using basically states that if 'many people' of a certain color commit a particular crime, it is only natural to associate (or suspect) everyone of that color with that same crime.

I want to ask you some questions: how many of you are afraid of white (American) men since most mass shootings in the US have been committed by white men?[1] How many of you have any trepidation investing into a company owned by a white (American) man since the majority of financial crimes in the US have been committed by college educated white men?[2] How many white men have you heard say that they have experienced discrimination in those aforementioned areas? I believe your (and my) answers to those questions are no. Therefore, why are people capable of not being suspicious of white people for crimes they predominantly commit, but incapable of doing the same for black people?

One reason is because when a white person does something bad, people see it as a **person** who did something bad, not a **white person**; their criminality is never linked to their color. Whereas, when black people (and people of other ethnicities) do bad things, people see it as a **black person** who did something bad, not a **person**; their criminality is linked to their color. In people's minds, black people are a community and share similar characteristics, and even some black people start to believe this idea.

A lot of black people have been implicitly told from a young age that we have this extremely negative identity. Some of us decide to take up this identity, but redefine it, to show the world that the 'black identity' is not negative at all. Unknowingly, by doing this, we are accepting the denial of our individuality and are bowing down to white privilege, to the idea that white people are the only individuals in this world. Since we have taken up this burden (because it is a burden) of the 'black identity', we feel responsible for every black person's behavior (and even if we don't, society would tell us that we are, looking to us to be knowledgeable about why this or that happens among some black people). Some of us feel that all black people should be working for the betterment of the image of the black man, and when a black person does something that 'drags our image in the mud', we feel ashamed, guilty, and critical of that person. I think the only time white people get this same sense of guilt is when people start talking about racism. Otherwise, I never hear white people act in any way responsible for the misdeeds of another white person or feel like they should all be working for the betterment of the image of the white man. And I never hear people see problems that happen predominantly among Whites as a sign of something being inherently wrong with white people. I have never heard people say that the hyper-sexualization of white female pop singers, models, and actresses shows that there is a problem with 'white culture'. I have never heard of people looking at young drug addicted white people and white males who go on shooting rampages as a sign of the moral failure of white families. White people are not asked to speak for 'the white community'. This is white privilege. White people **should** be treated as individuals, and so **should everyone else** from every color under the sun.

So one technique I use to see black people as individuals is that when I hear of white people doing bad things, I ask myself this question, "Did they do this because they are white?" or I say, "This is a *white* person behaving badly, now if this had been a *black* person, would I link their bad behavior to their color?". When I hear of black people doing bad things, I have to constantly remind myself that white people (and other 'races') have also done similar things. What this does is that it continuously reminds me that since I do not associate the skin color of white people with the mistakes of some white people, there is therefore no logic in associating the color of black people with the mistakes of some black people.

Finally, the 'black identity' has become a refuge for me and many other black people. With this 'identity', a lot of us now protect and defend one another from racism; and I believe that this is very important. Black people (and Biracials) need safe spaces to call our own. We need spaces that are free from the constant onslaught of racist ideas and discrimination, spaces that promote and treasure our physical, cultural and historical differences which are often insulted and pushed aside. We need spaces that do not deny or brush aside the various types of black experiences due to racism. Nevertheless, while we rest in these safe spaces, we need to keep in mind that we are all individuals, and that these safe spaces were created because of racial discrimination, not because black people are a community that share some form of familial bond or similar characteristics and beliefs. We need to not be shocked when we see and read of black people behaving in ways that are different from us. Why wouldn't they? We are all individuals.

Racism is not the Almighty

Lastly, as we fight against racial injustice within ourselves and out in the world, we may feel hopeless and tired, but despite what happens, let us always keep in mind and on our lips phrases like, "racism and racial injustice will not win", "justice will prevail", or words that definitively state that racism will not be victorious. The reason I say this is because racism is not some great, big undefeatable demon in the sky that can't be brought down. It was brought down with the end of the Transatlantic and Arab slave trade, with the abolition of slavery, the civil rights movement in the US, with the end of colonization around the world, and with the end of apartheid in South Africa. Racism and white supremacy have been defeated time and time again, so let us not see it in our minds or paint it with our words as an undefeated champion nor surround ourselves with stories where it prevailed so that we don't lose the strength to fight against it. Remember, the battle is in the mind. No matter how we feel and no matter what happens out in the world, let us never put racism on a pedestal. It may win some battles, but we will win the war. Let us not lose hope; instead let us push for a change in our own thoughts, beliefs, and actions and as we make an effort to change ourselves, we stand to change those around us, who then stand to change those around them and the cycle goes on until racism is defeated around the world.

9 CONCLUSION

I wrote this book to help people fight against racism in their lives, specifically implicit racism. I hope this book has opened your eyes to understand that racism is not a problem that only exists in other people's lives, but is something that we too have to fight against within ourselves. I shared openly about my experiences with racism to help remove the stigma that being called a racist carries. I am optimistic that by sharing my experience, it will pave the way for others to be willing to acknowledge their own internal struggles with racism.

I have armed you with the knowledge of how implicit racist ideas are spread so that you will no longer be unaware of the effects these ideas have on your thoughts, beliefs, and actions. As you apply the techniques I have given here, I pray you don't give up no matter how long it takes to see progress in your thoughts and beliefs. Remember that racist beliefs were not formed in a day, nor will it take a day to remove them. But I believe that as you continue to persevere in this fight against racist ideas in your mind, you will eventually overcome them because I am living proof that you can have victory over explicit and implicit racist beliefs.

Thank you for reading this book. If this book has touched you, please consider telling your family, friends, and acquaintances about it. And please consider leaving a review on different online stores.

ABOUT THE AUTHOR

Sefunmi Oladumiye is a fantasy fiction writer who has quite a few fantasy story ideas floating around in her mind, so you can imagine her surprise that her first published work is a non-fiction book.

Sefunmi grew up wanting to be a fiction writer and was always retelling stories she had heard to anyone who would listen. She gave up this dream in high school because she felt that she didn't know how to put her ideas into words. However, story ideas didn't give up on her and began to flood her mind during her university days. This made her realize that she had to write. She hopes to finally publish some of her fantasy fiction work in 2017.

She currently lives in Nigeria, loves chocolate, fantasy books, and reading on cloudy or rainy days.
You can visit her online to find out about her upcoming books:

    Facebook- Sefunmi Oladumiye
    Website –mebooksblog.wordpress.com
    Twitter - @sefunmioladumiA

NOTES

Chapter 1:
1.Gannon, Megan. "Race Is a Social Construct, Scientists Argue". *Scientific American.* Springer Nature, 5 Feb 2016. Web. 21 February 2017.
Chapter 4:
1. "Prejudice." Def.1.*Cambridge Dictionary*, Cambridge University Press, n.d. Web. 22 Feb. 2017.
2."Discrimination." Def.1. *English Oxford Living Dictionaries*. Oxford University Press, n.d. Web. 22 Feb. 2017.
3. "Racism." Def.1. *English Oxford Living Dictionaries*. Oxford University Press, n.d. Web. 22 Feb. 2017.
4. "Colourism." Def.1. *English Oxford Living Dictionaries*. Oxford University Press, n.d. Web. 22 Feb. 2017.
5. Zimmermann, Kim A. "What is Culture?" *Live Science*. Purch, 19 Feb 2015.Web. 22 Nov 2016.
6. "What is society'?." *Reference*. IAC Publishing, n.d.Web. 22 Nov 2016.
Chapter 5:
1. Adichie, Chimamanda N. "The Danger of a Single Story."TED. Oct. 2009. Lecture.
Chapter 7:
1. Holman Christian Standard Bible version
2. New International Version
3. Kahn, Andrew and Kirk, Chris. "What It's Like to Be Black in the Criminal Justice System." *Slate*. The Slate Group, 9 Aug 2015. Web. 24 Feb 2017
Chapter 8:
1. **"Number of mass shootings in the United States between 1982 and 2016, by mass shooter's race and ethnicity."** *The Statistics Portal*. Statista, June 2016. Web. 24 Feb 2017
2. Gerencher, Kristen. "Skimming from the top." *Market watch*. Market watch, 18 July 2001. Web. 24 Feb 2017

Manufactured by Amazon.ca
Bolton, ON